backyard winter

widarto adi

To purchase or licence images / prints please contact
dartophoto@gmail.com

ISBN-13: 978-1507547533

ISBN-10: 1507547536

Printed by CreateSpace, An Amazon.com Company

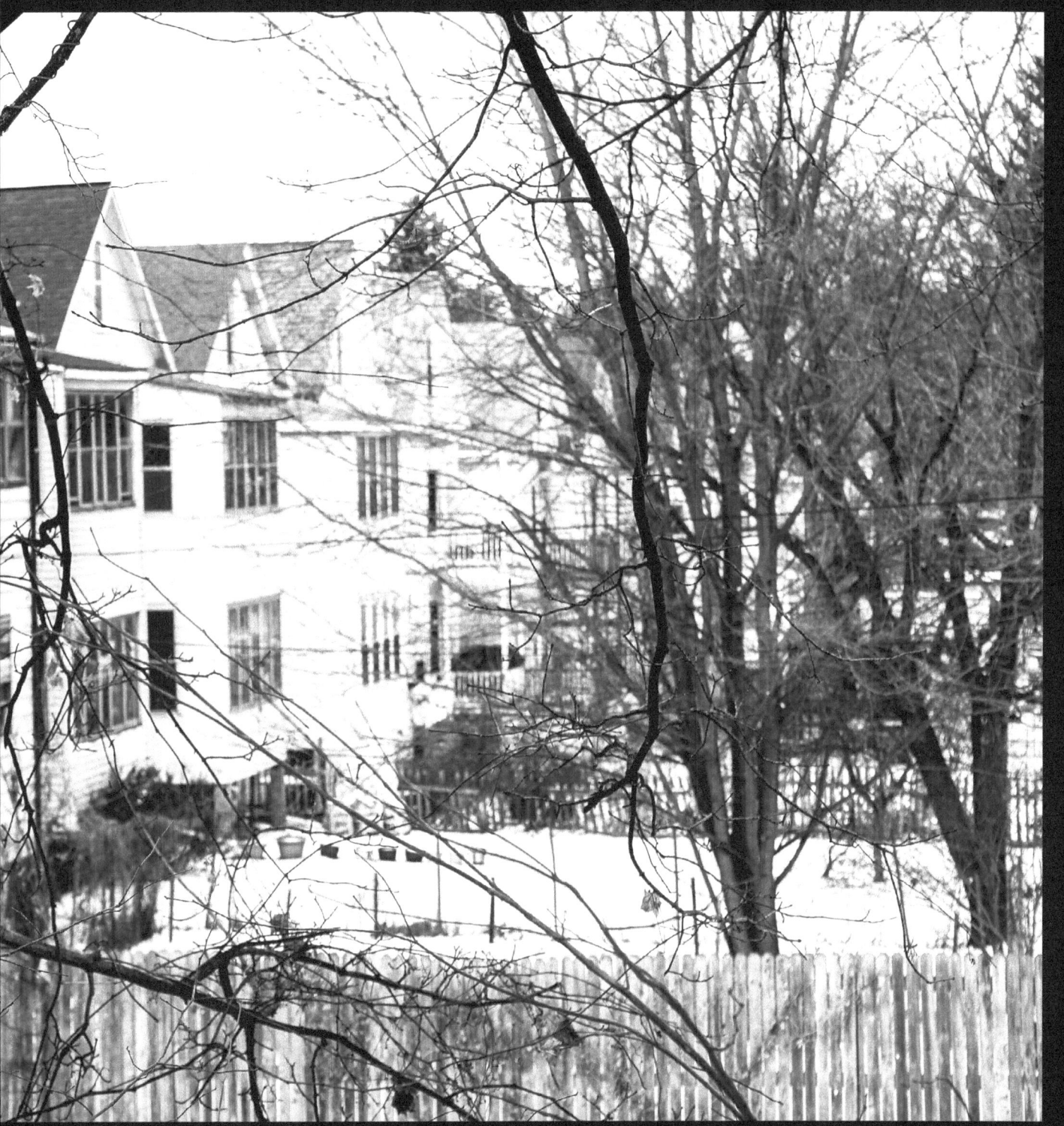

Come close to me, oh companion of my full life;
Come close to me and let not Winter's touch Enter between us.
Sit by me before the hearth,
For fire is the only fruit of Winter.

The Life Of Love XVI
Khalil Gibran

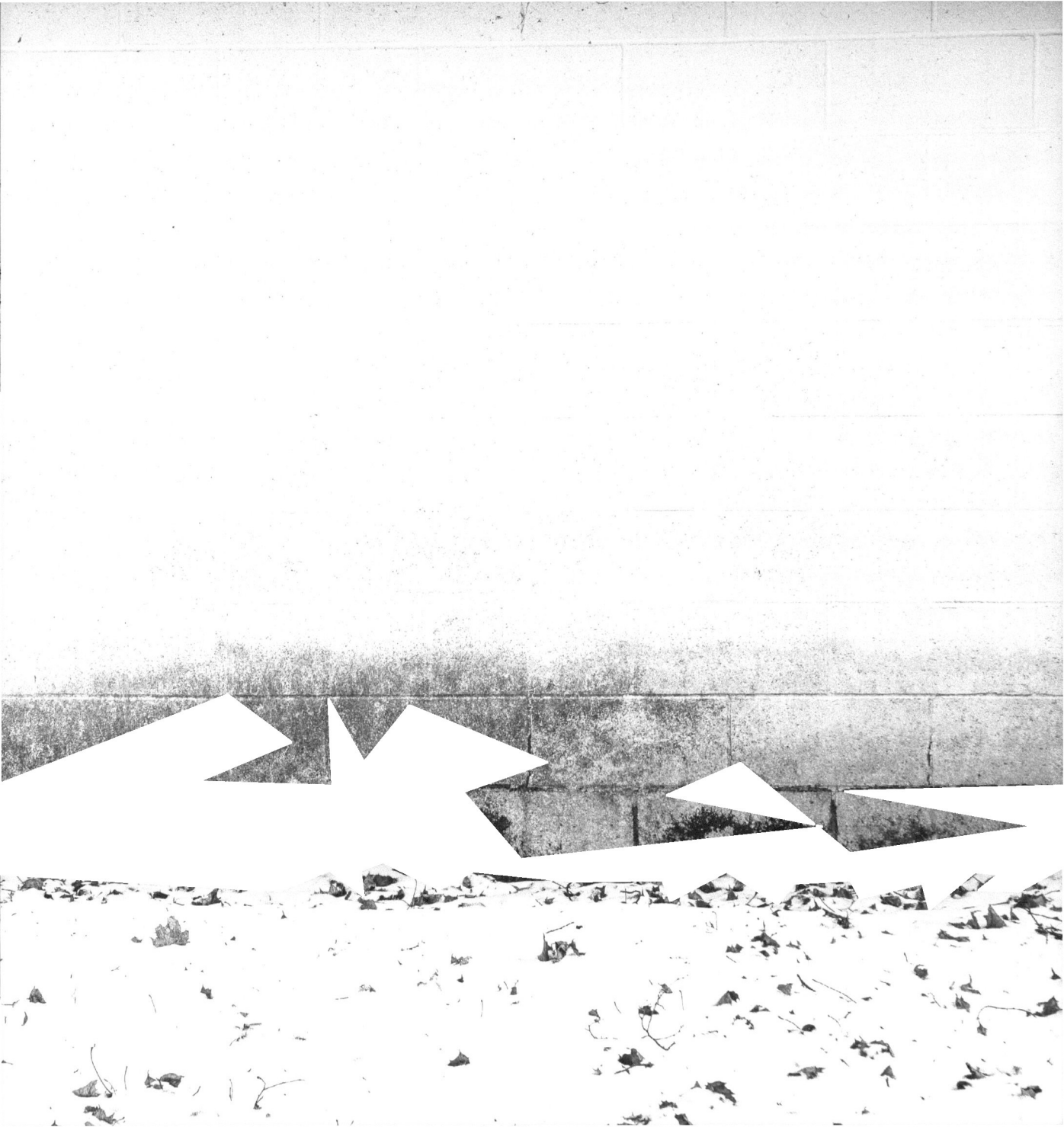

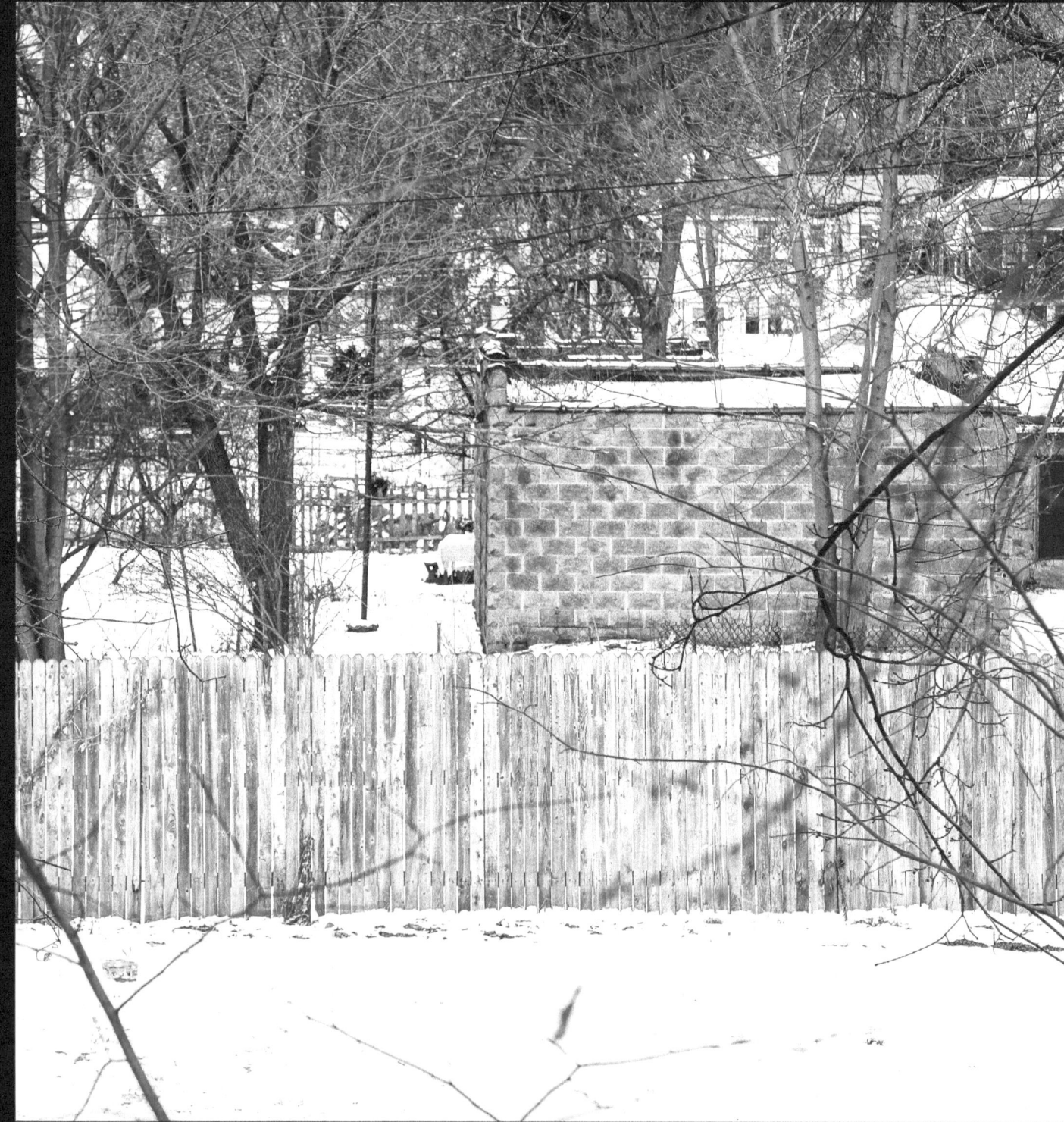

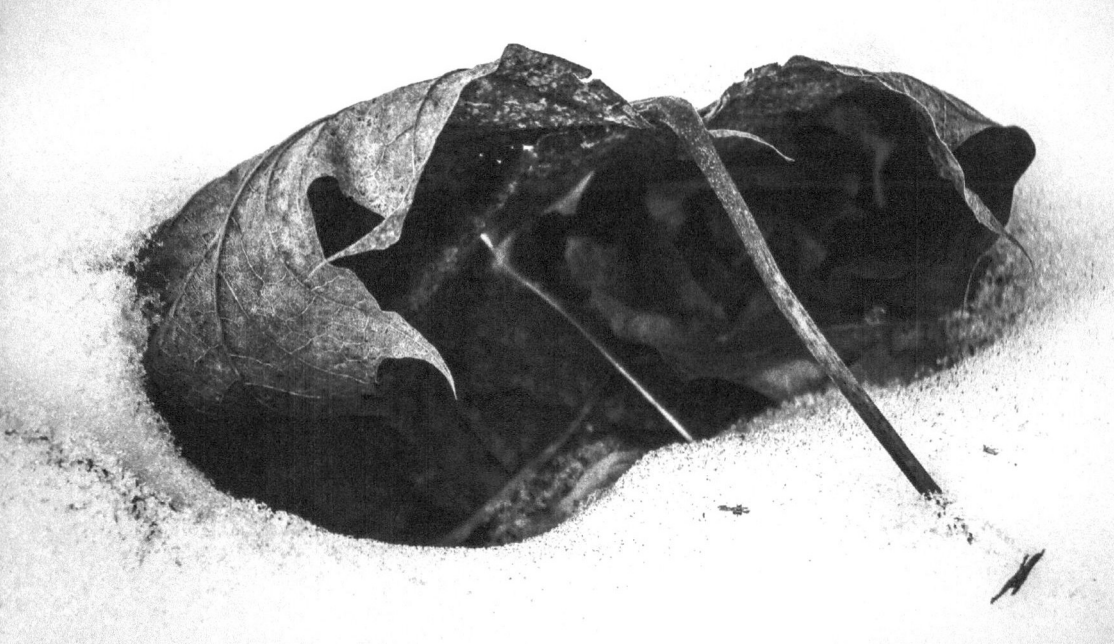

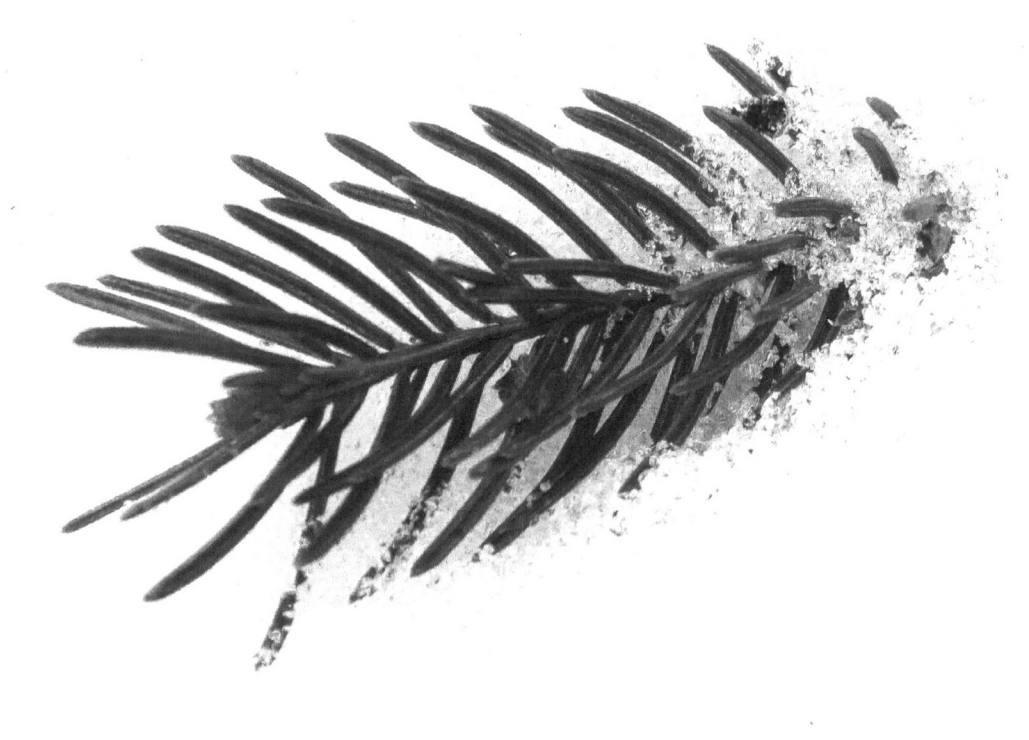

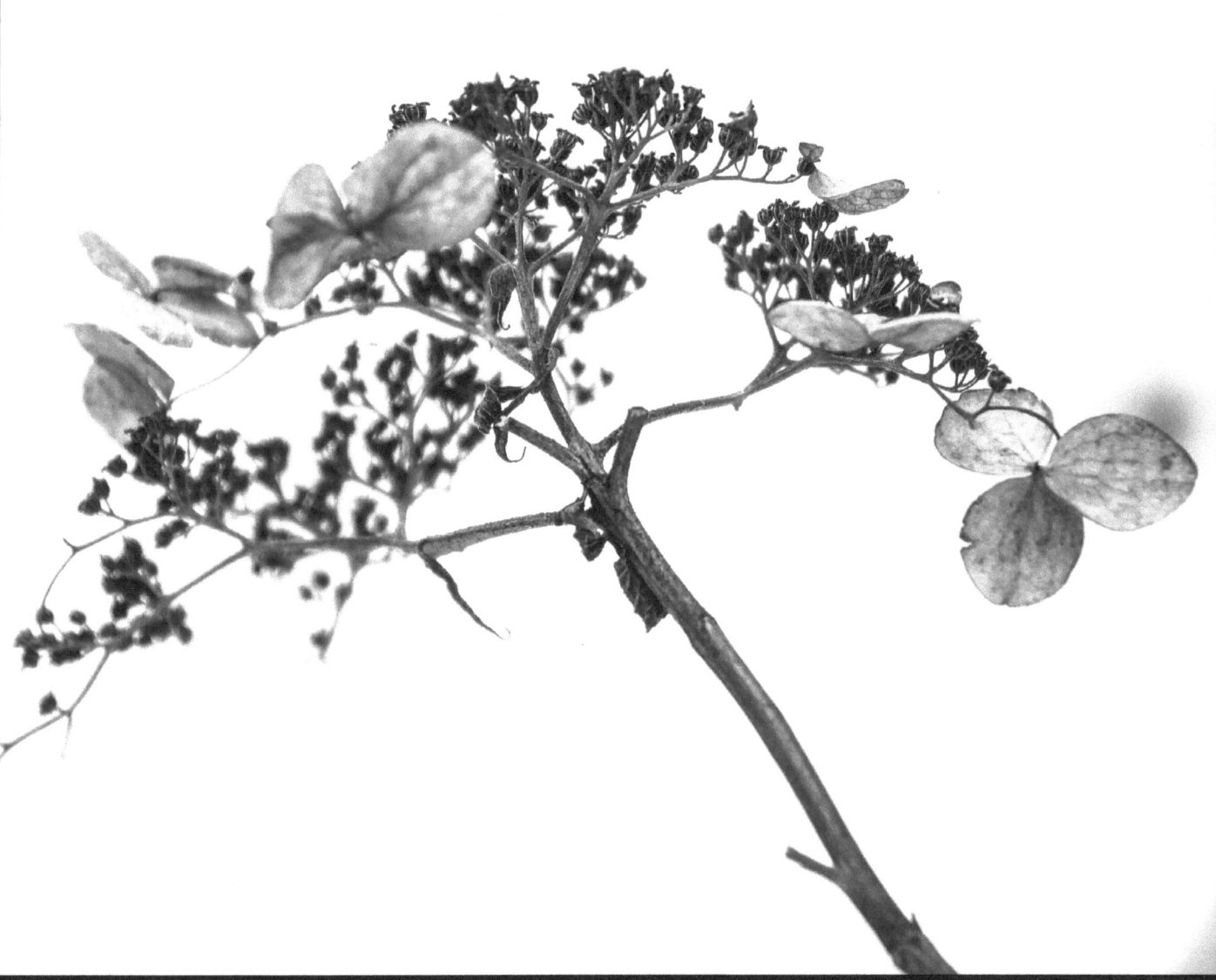

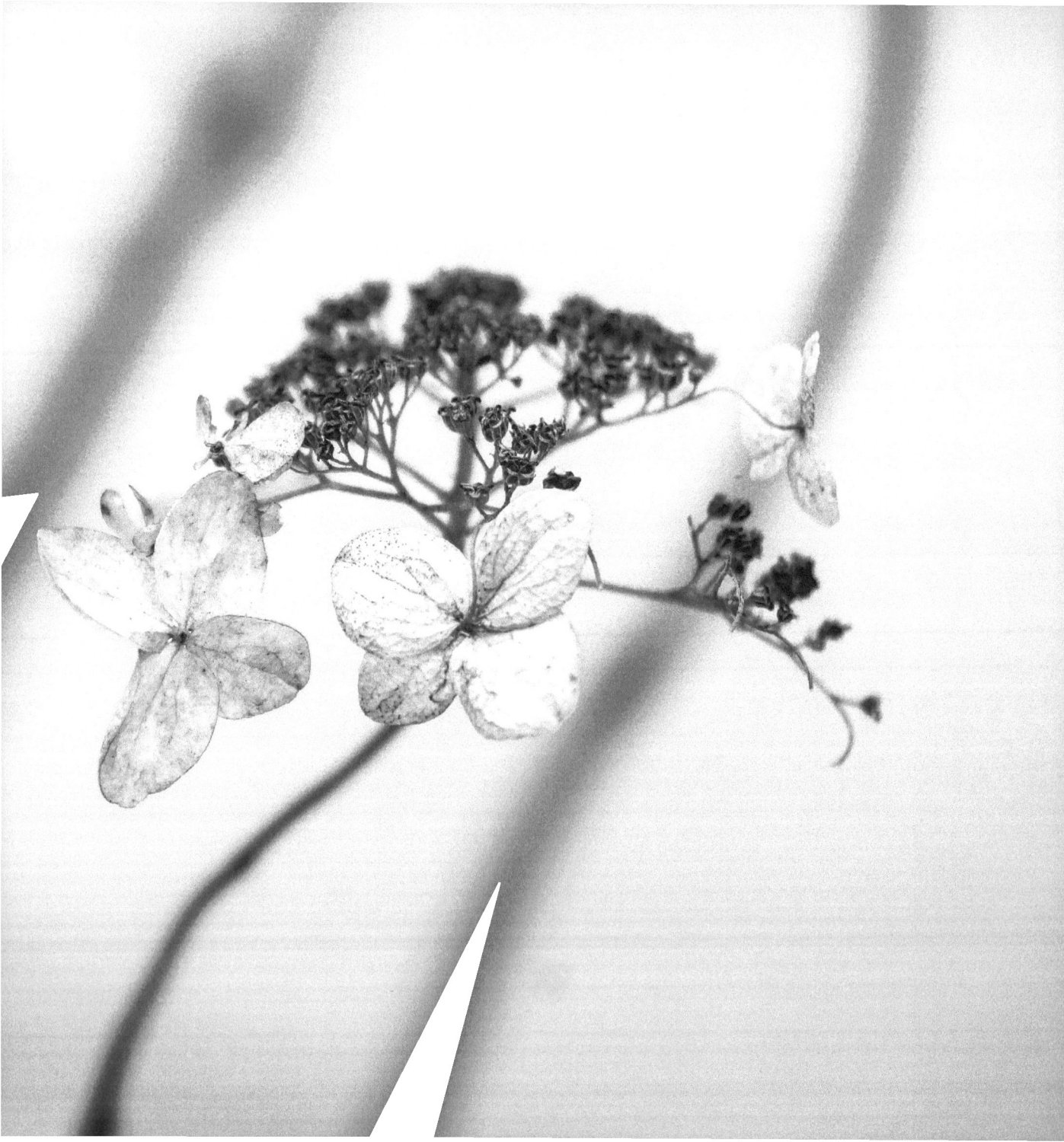

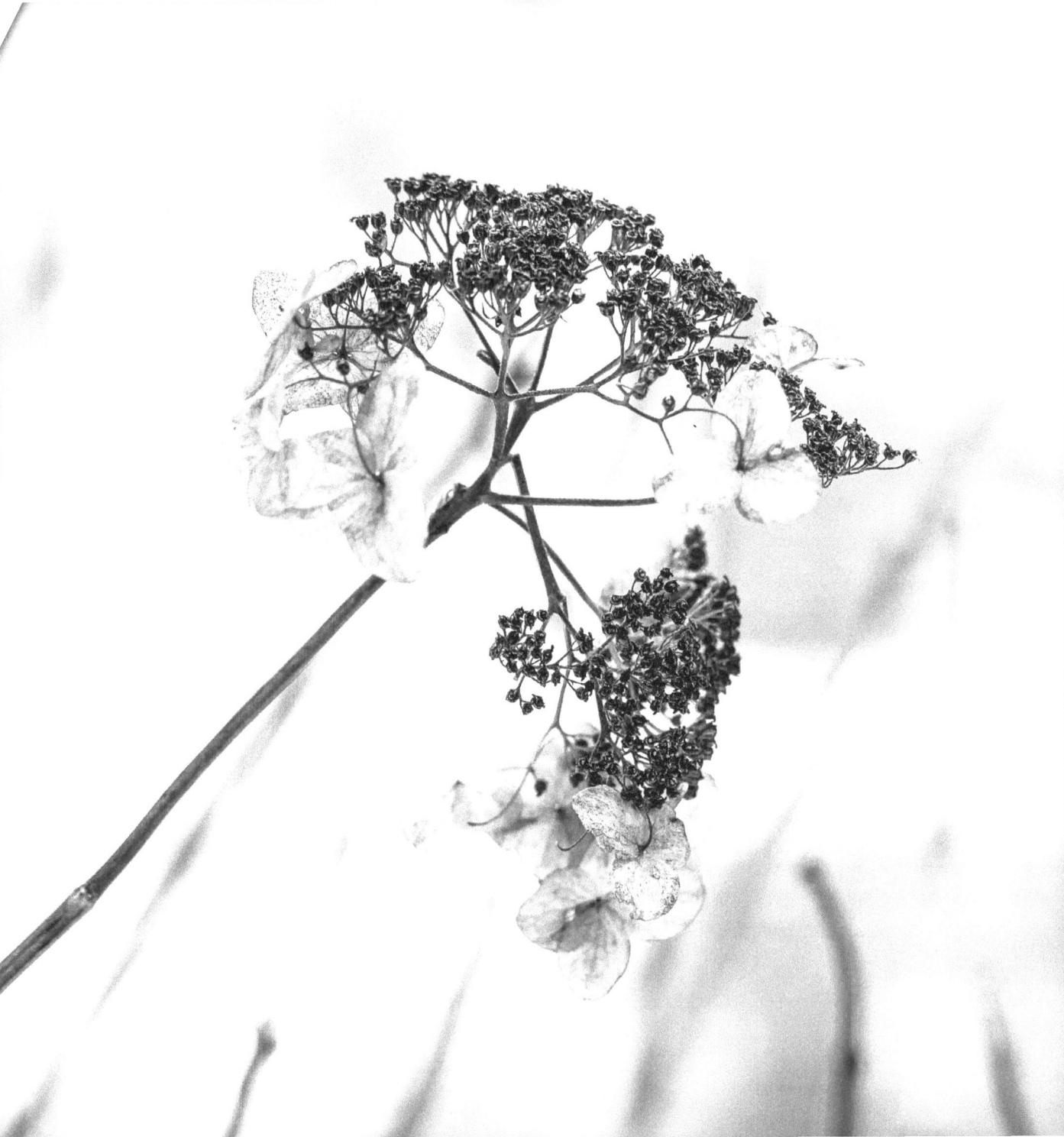

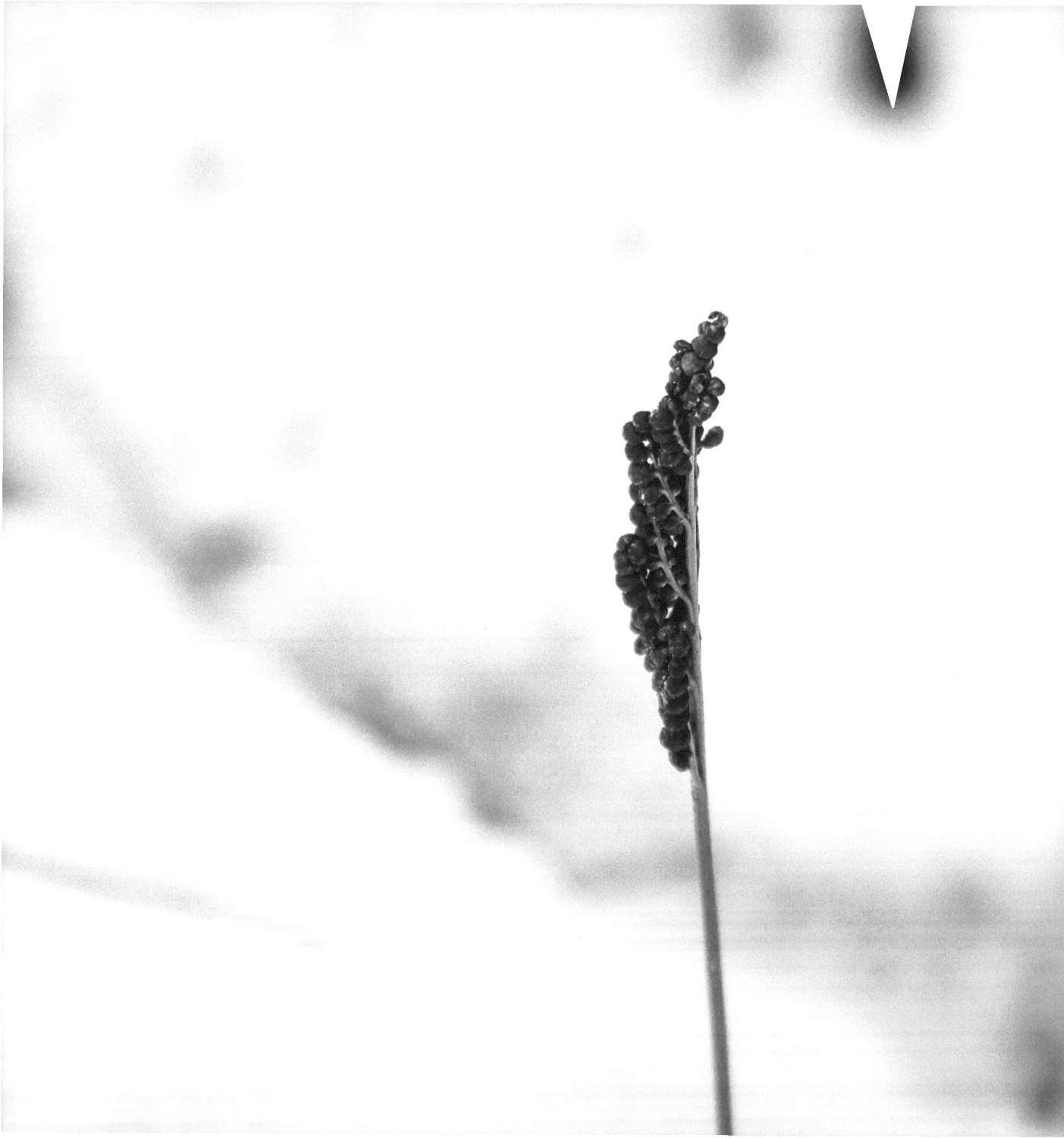

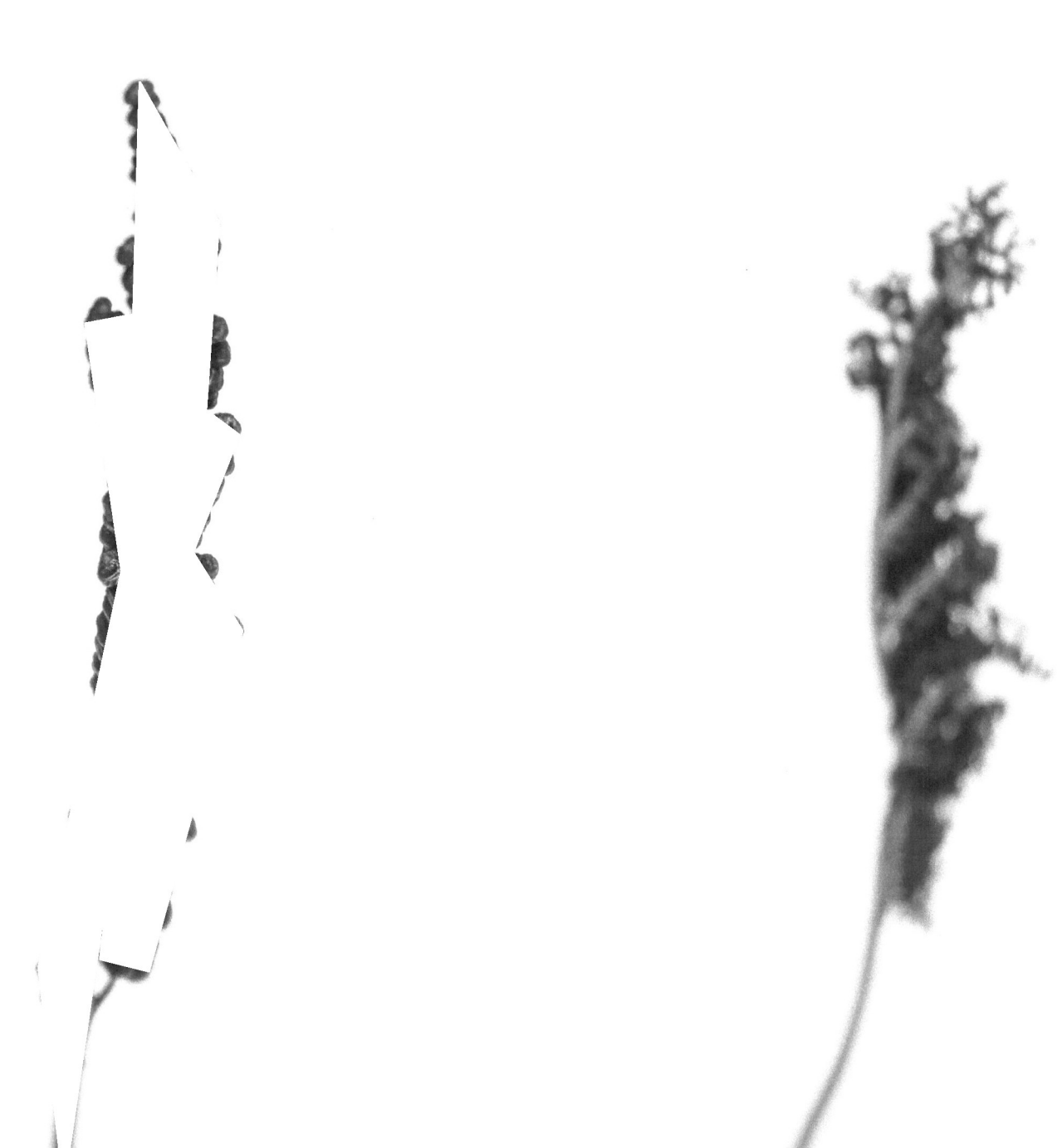

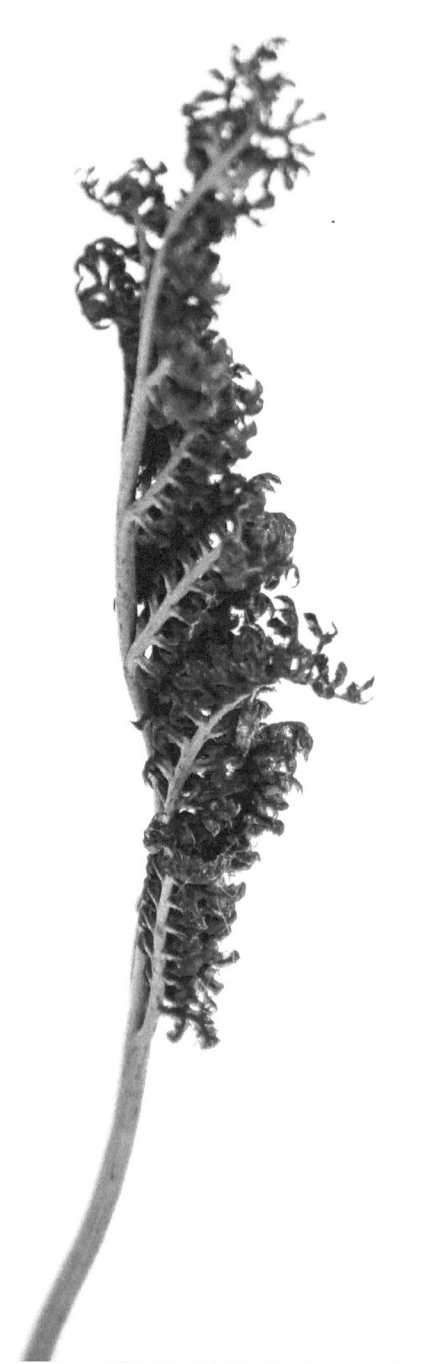

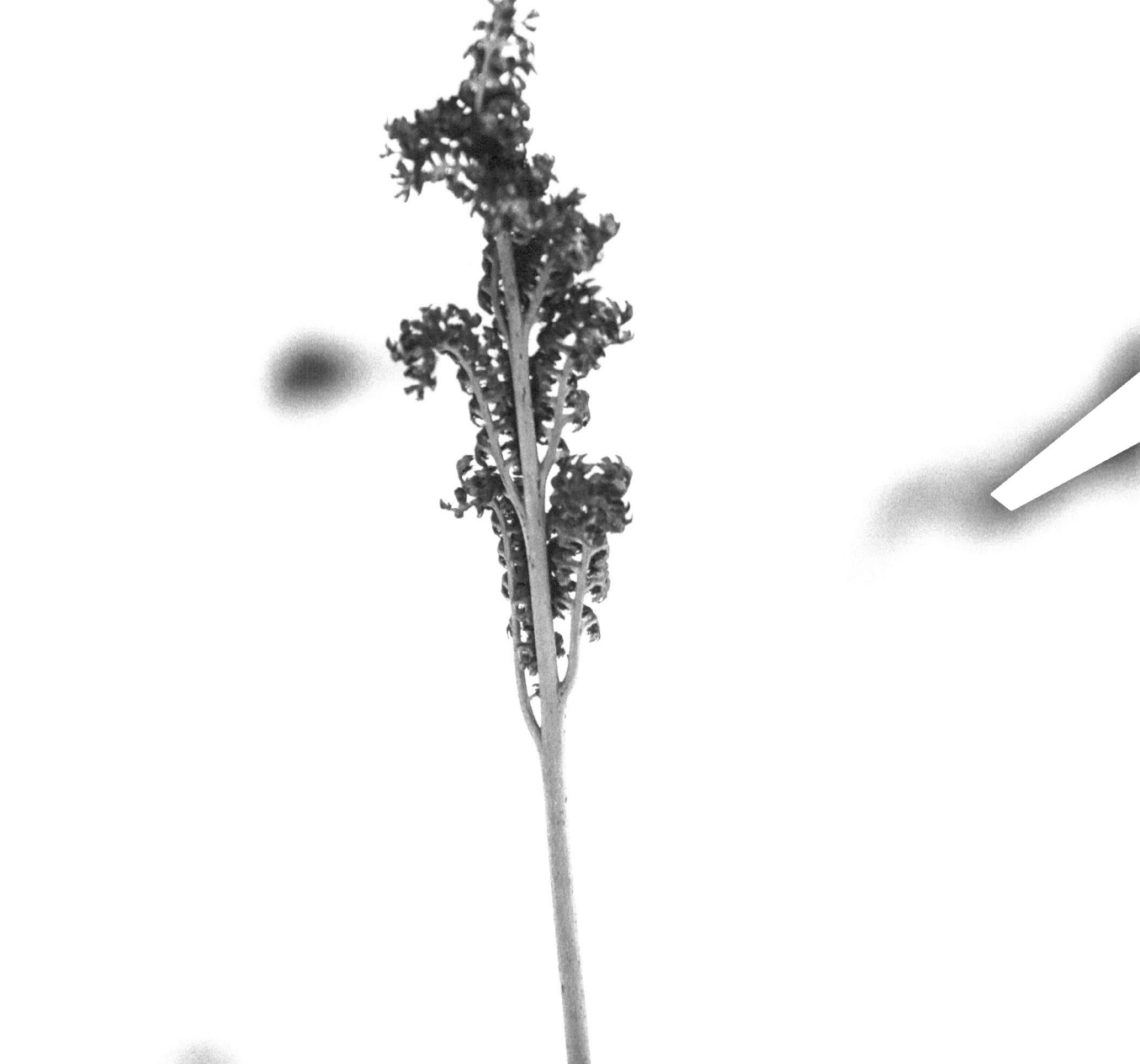

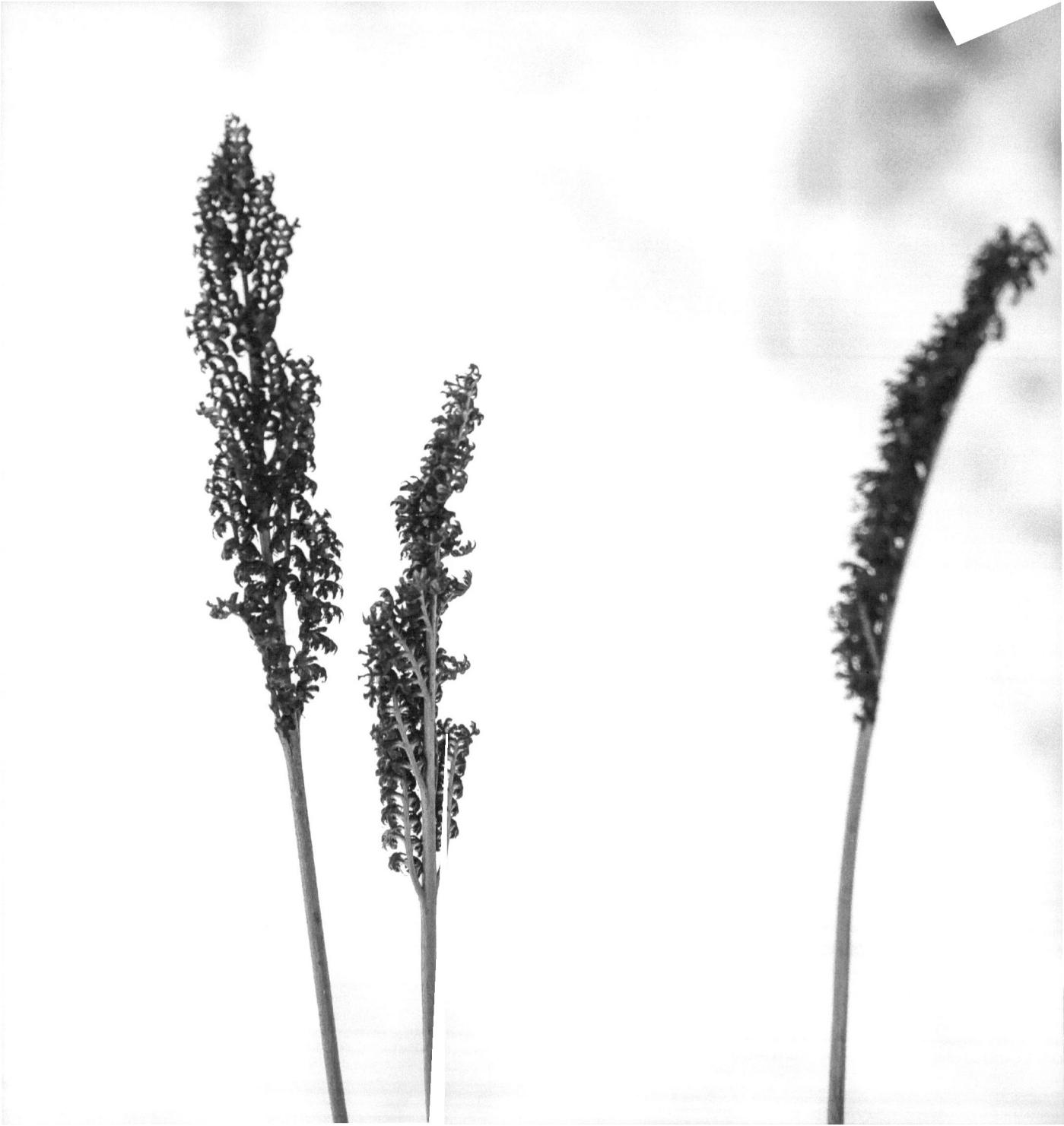

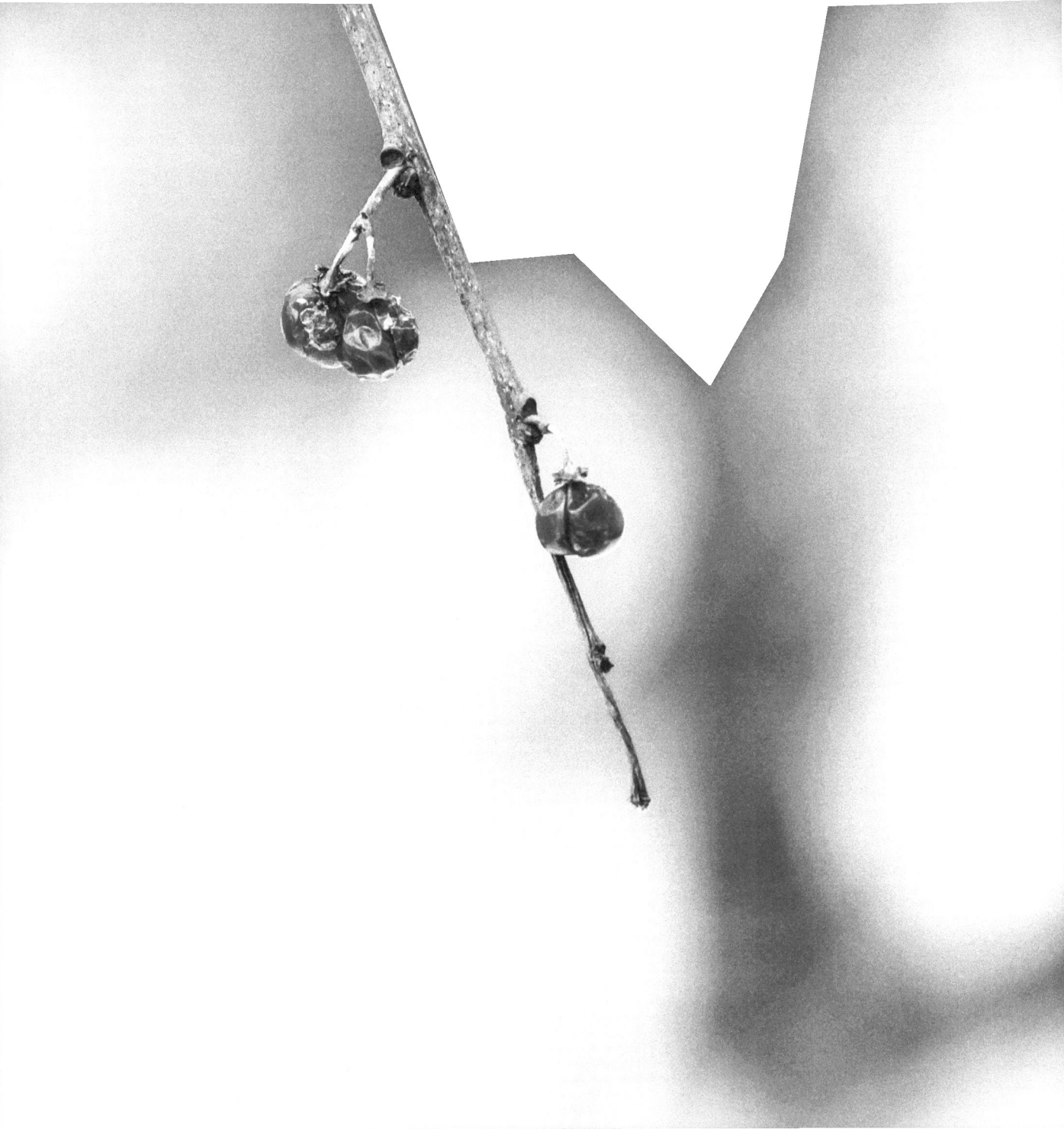

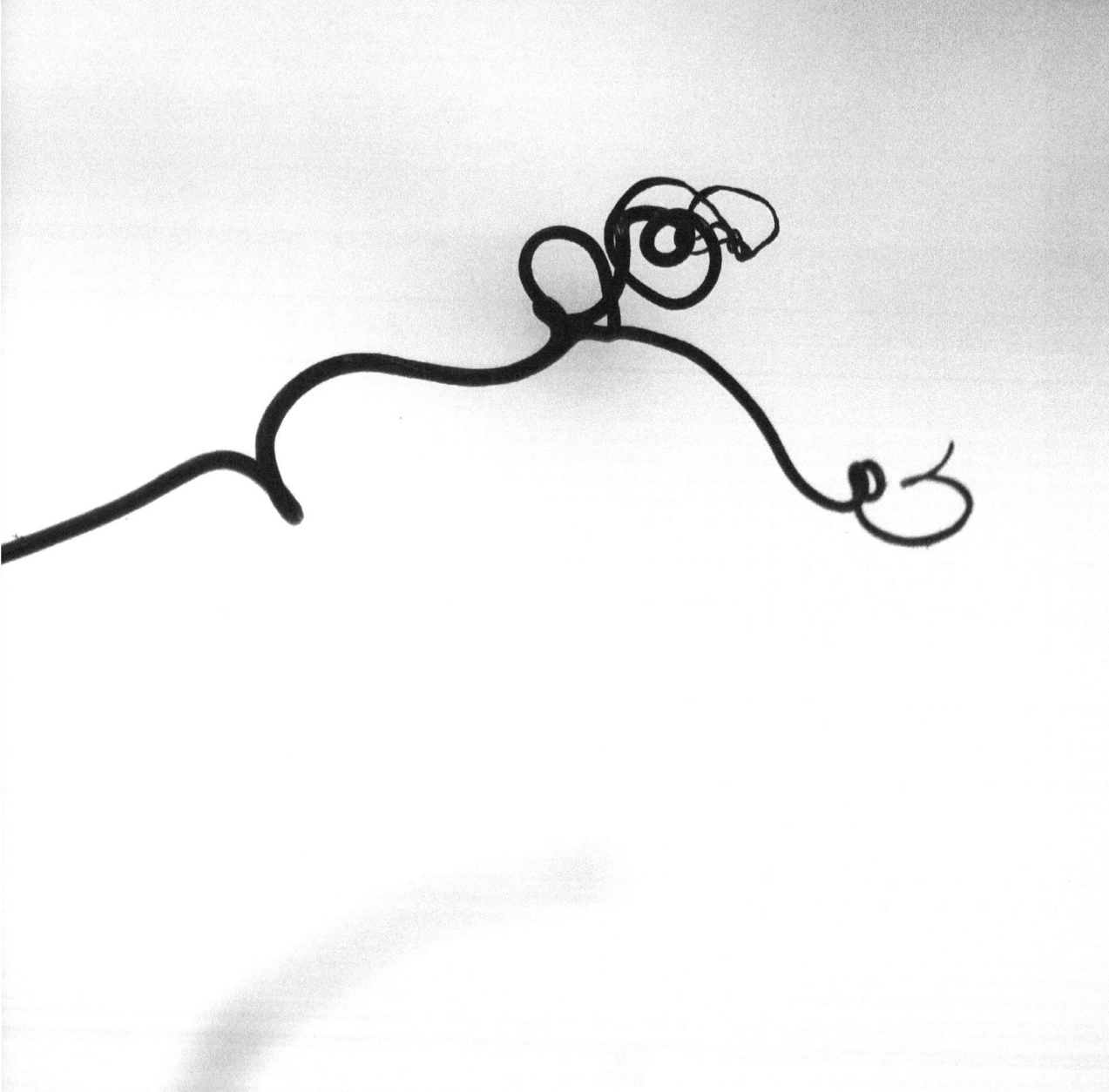

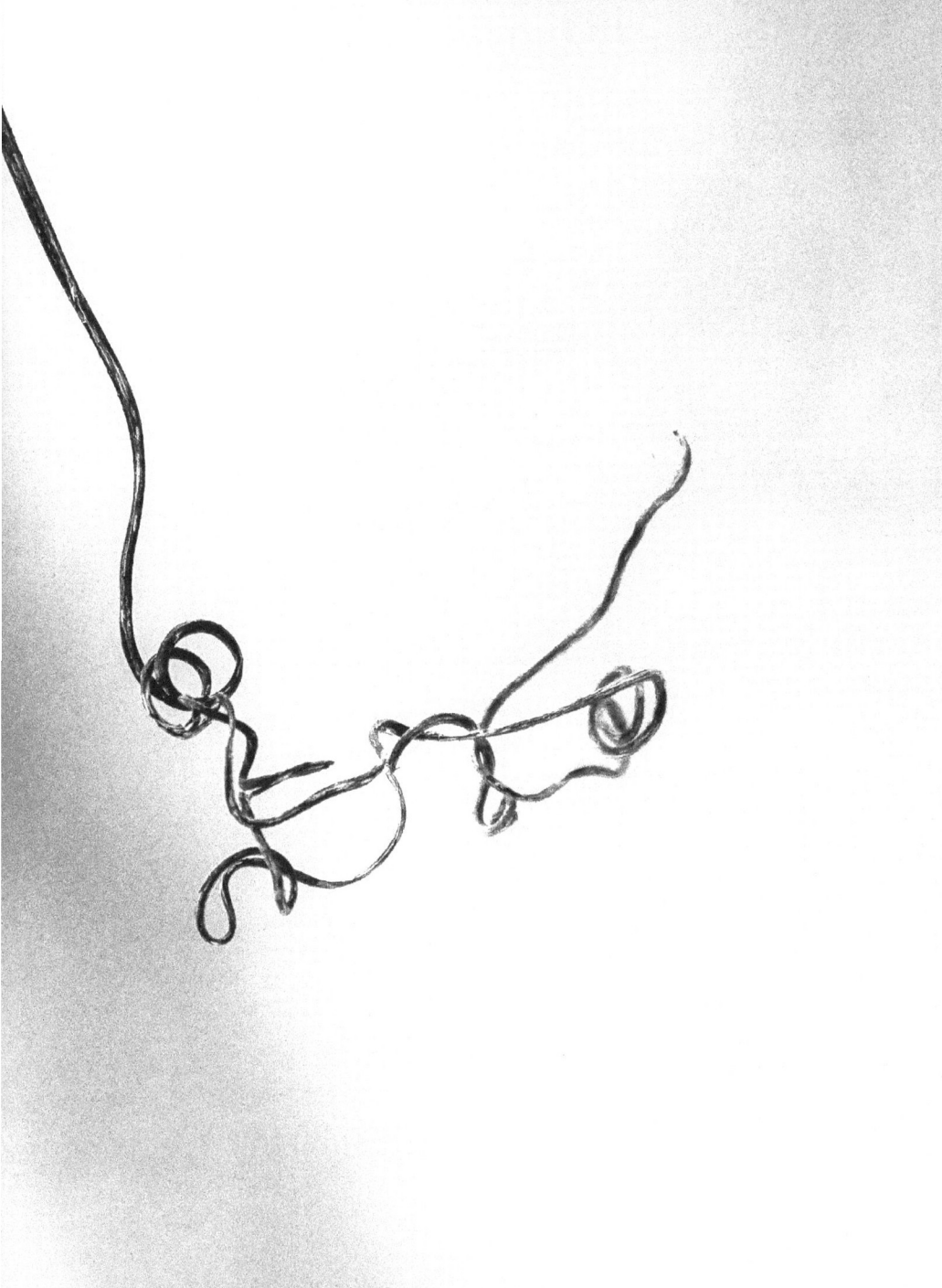

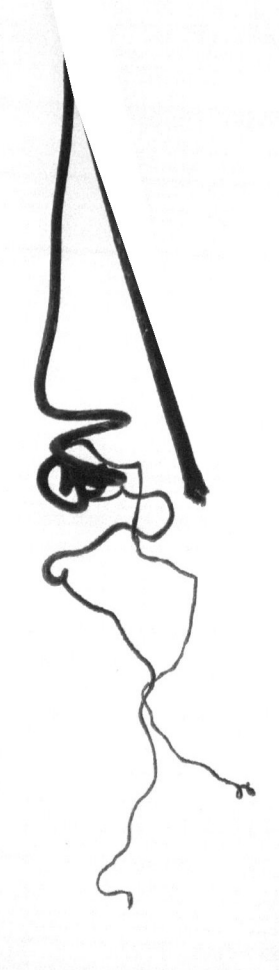

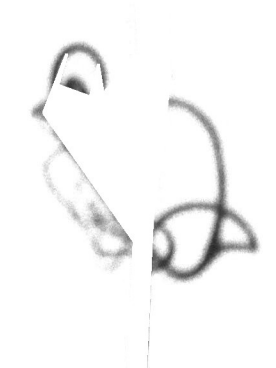

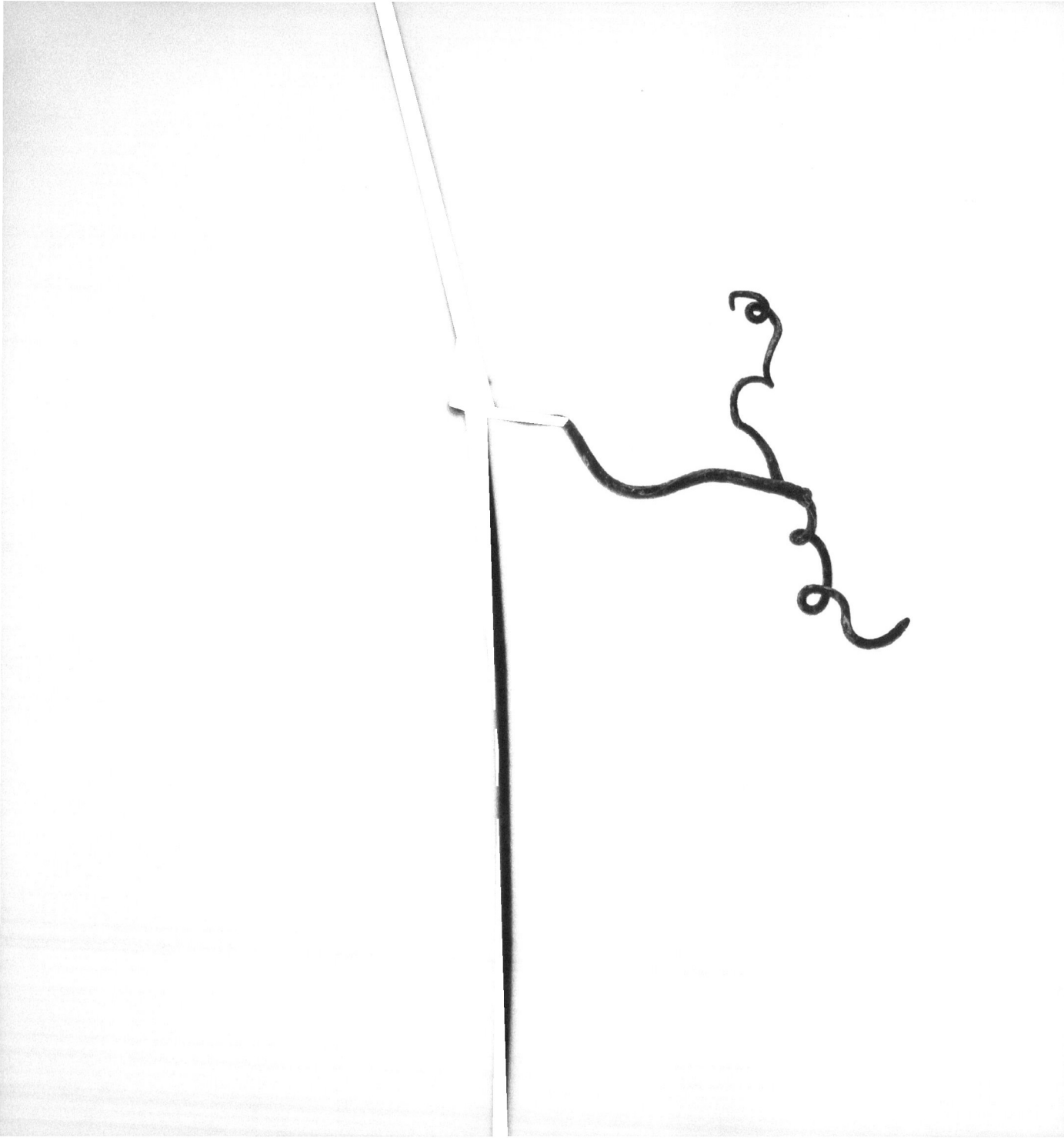

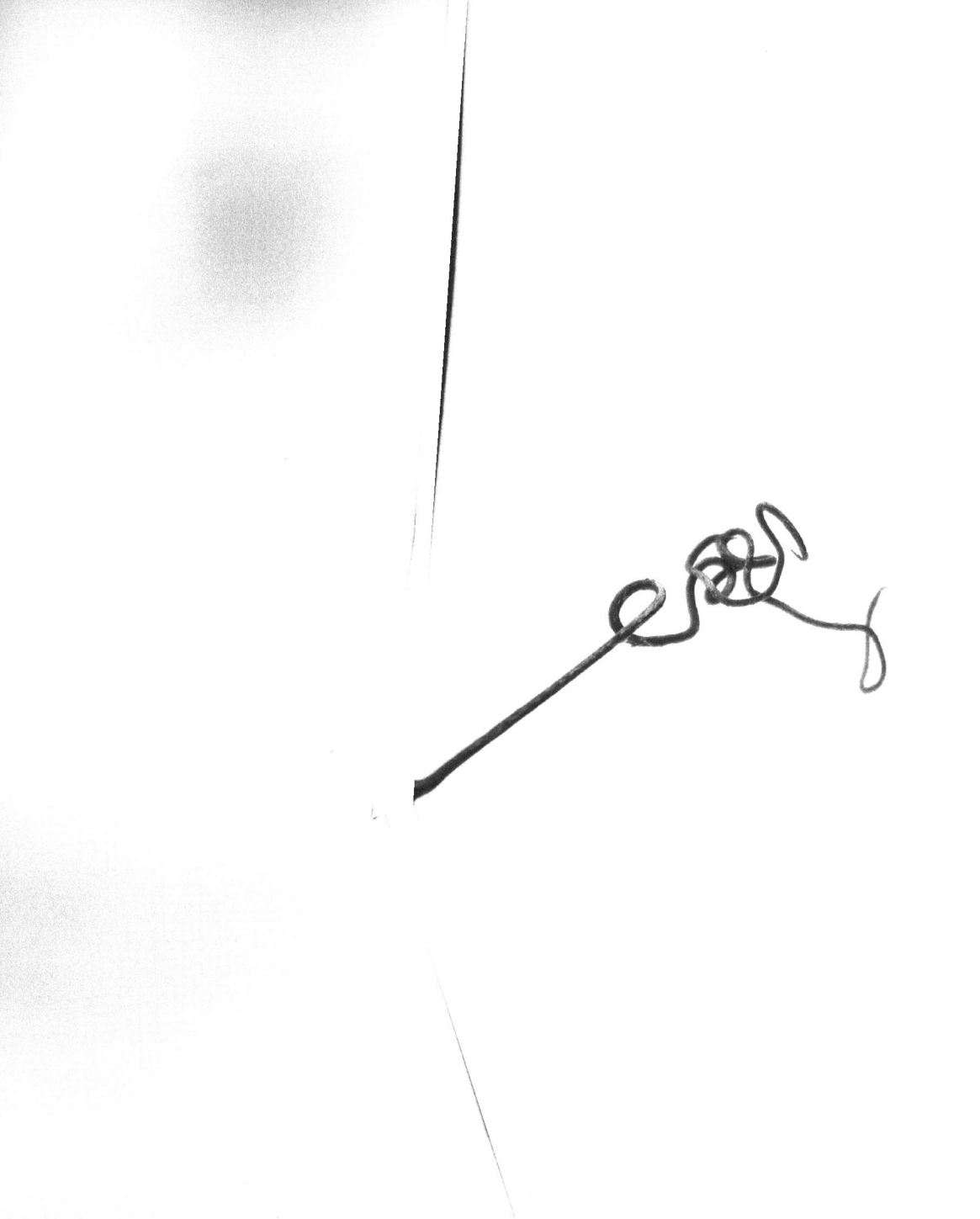

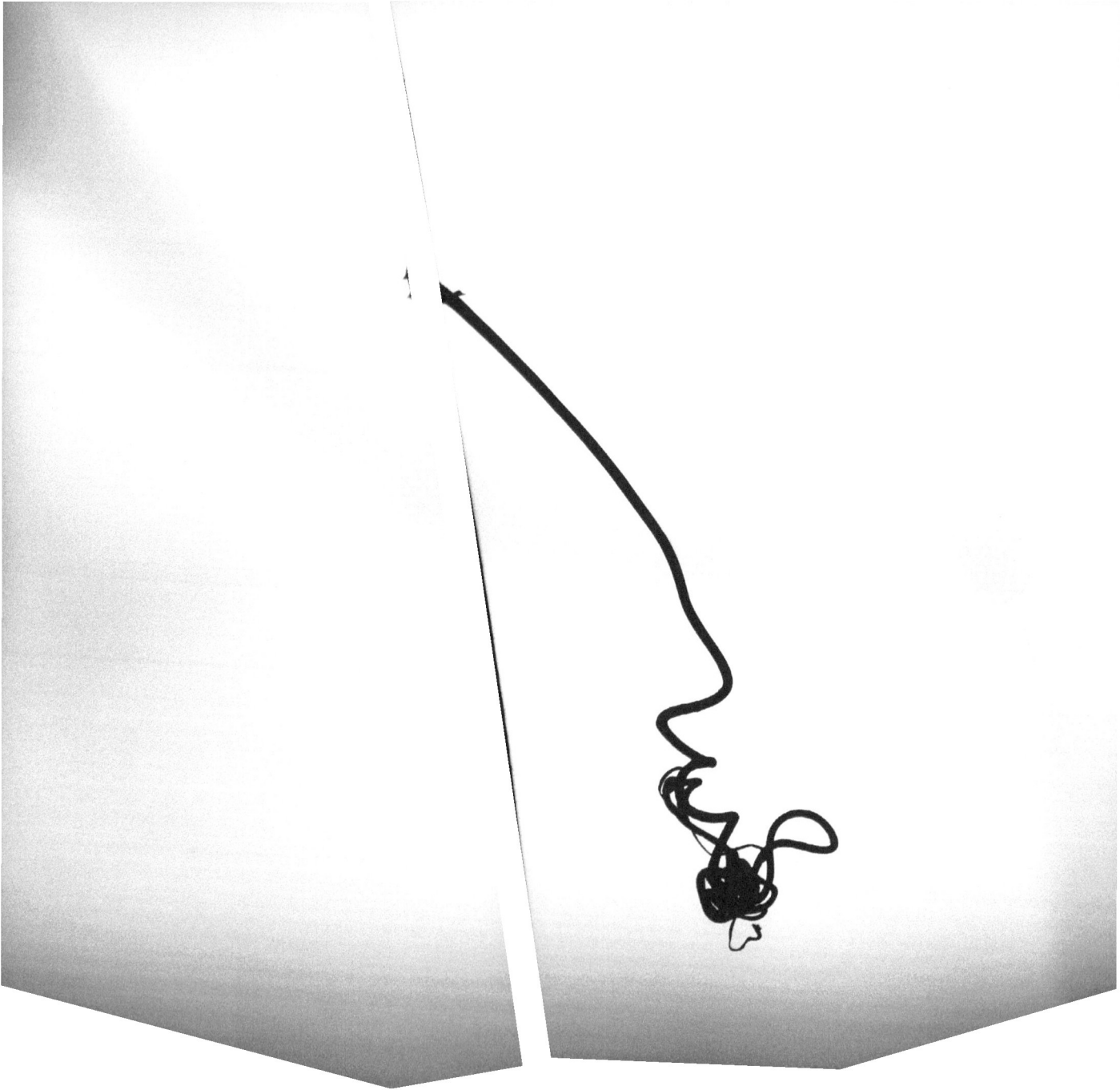

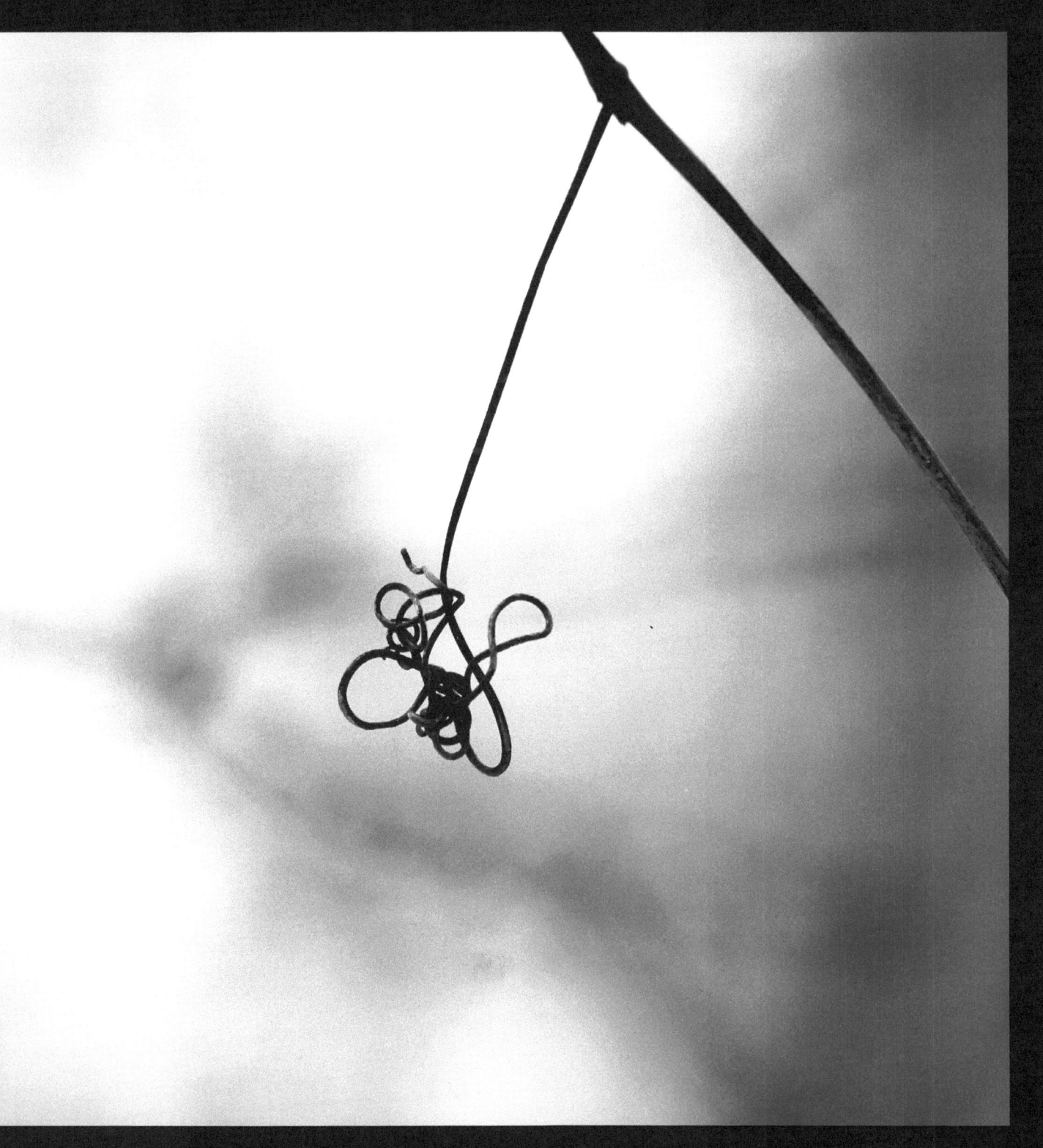

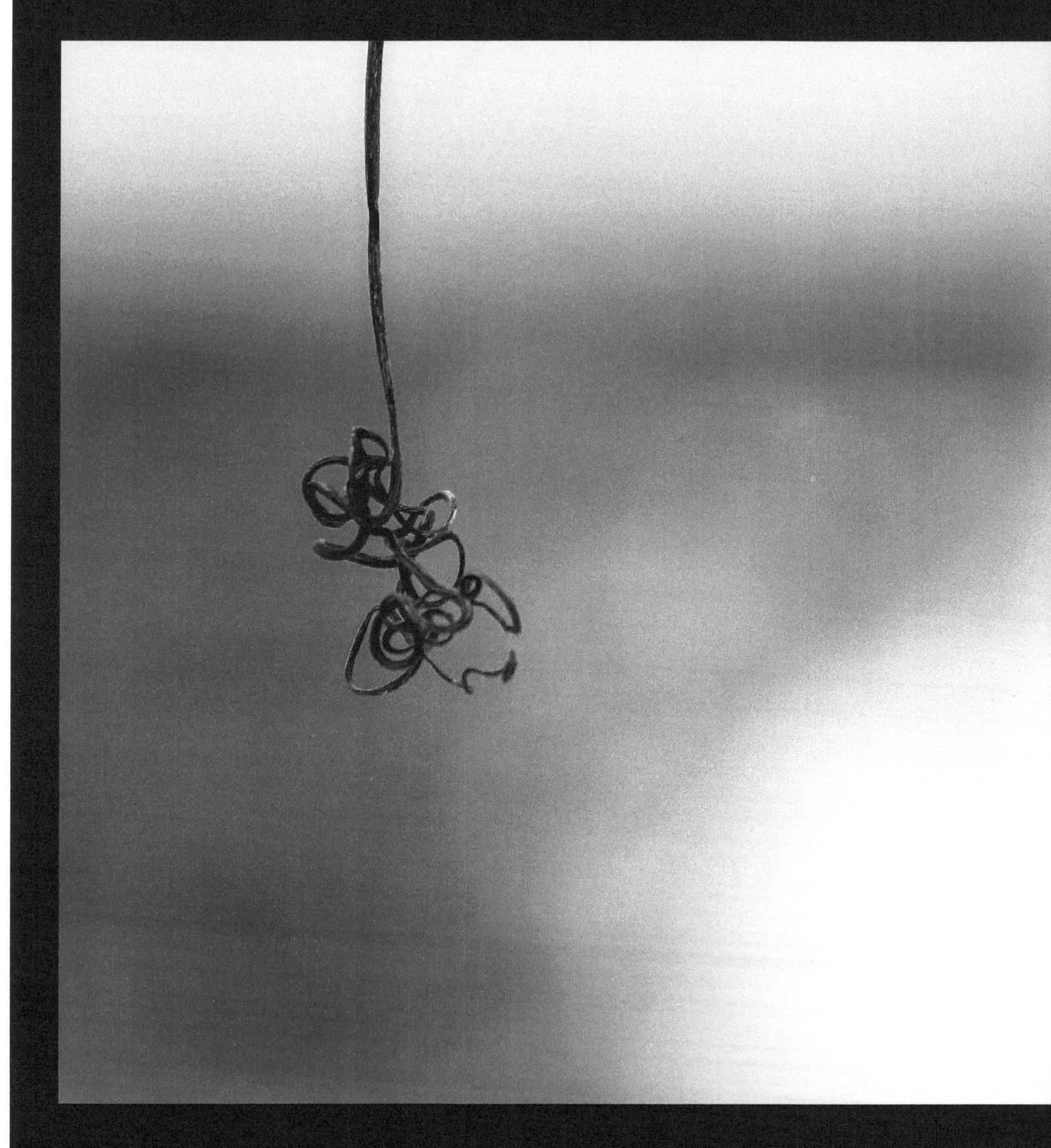

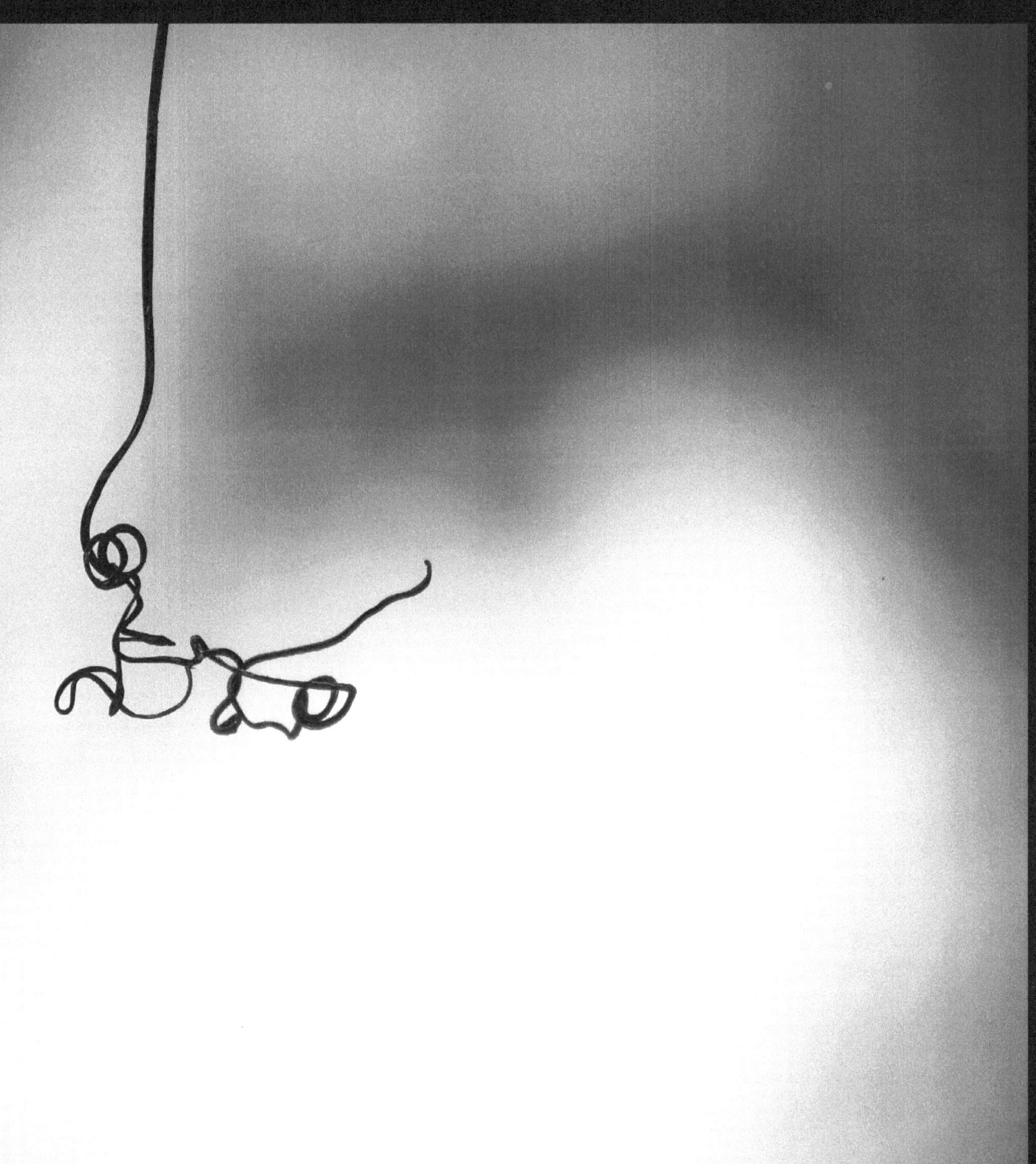

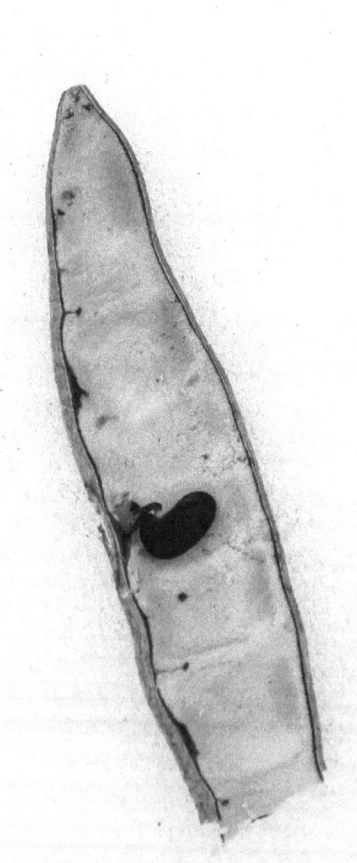

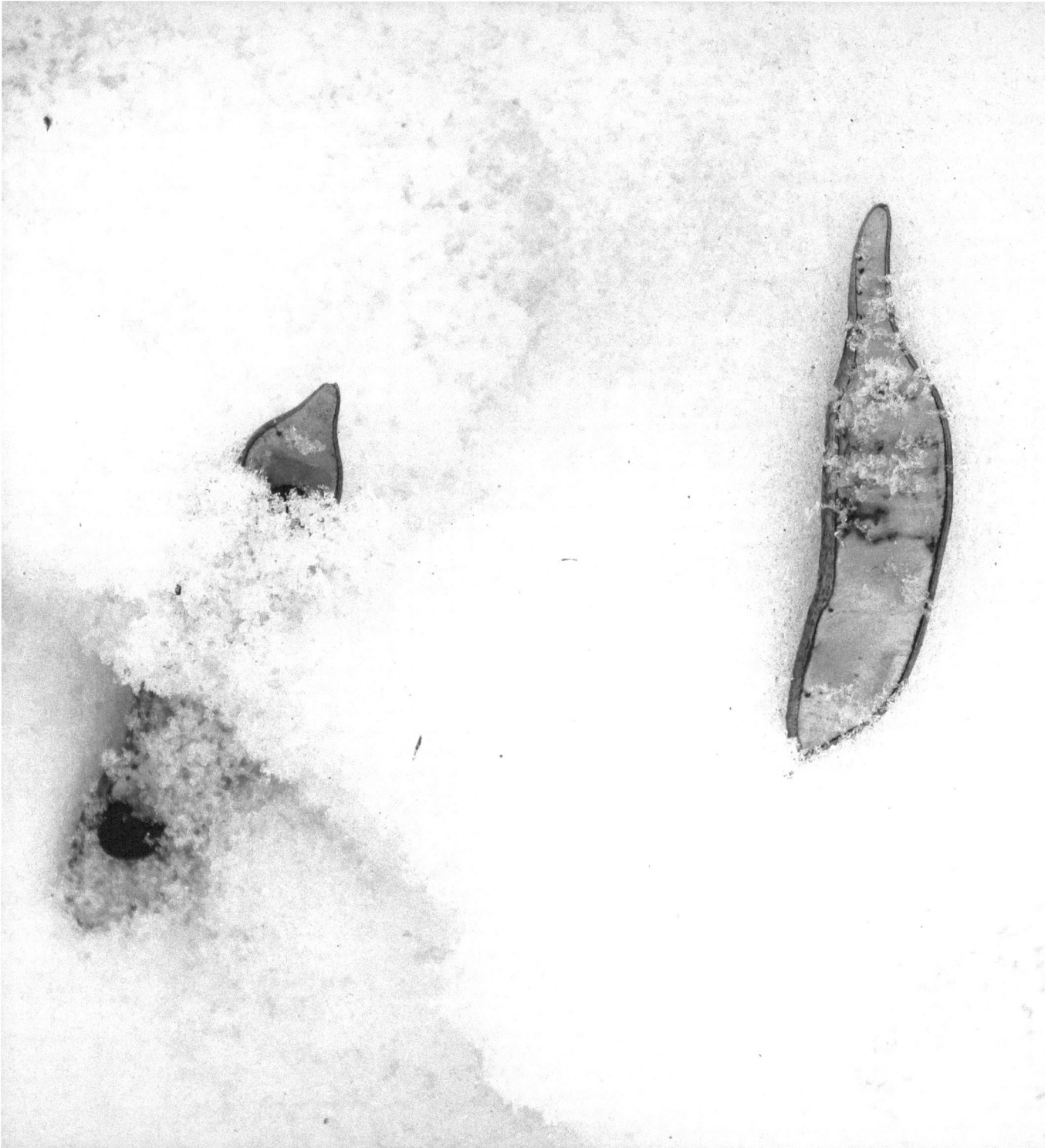

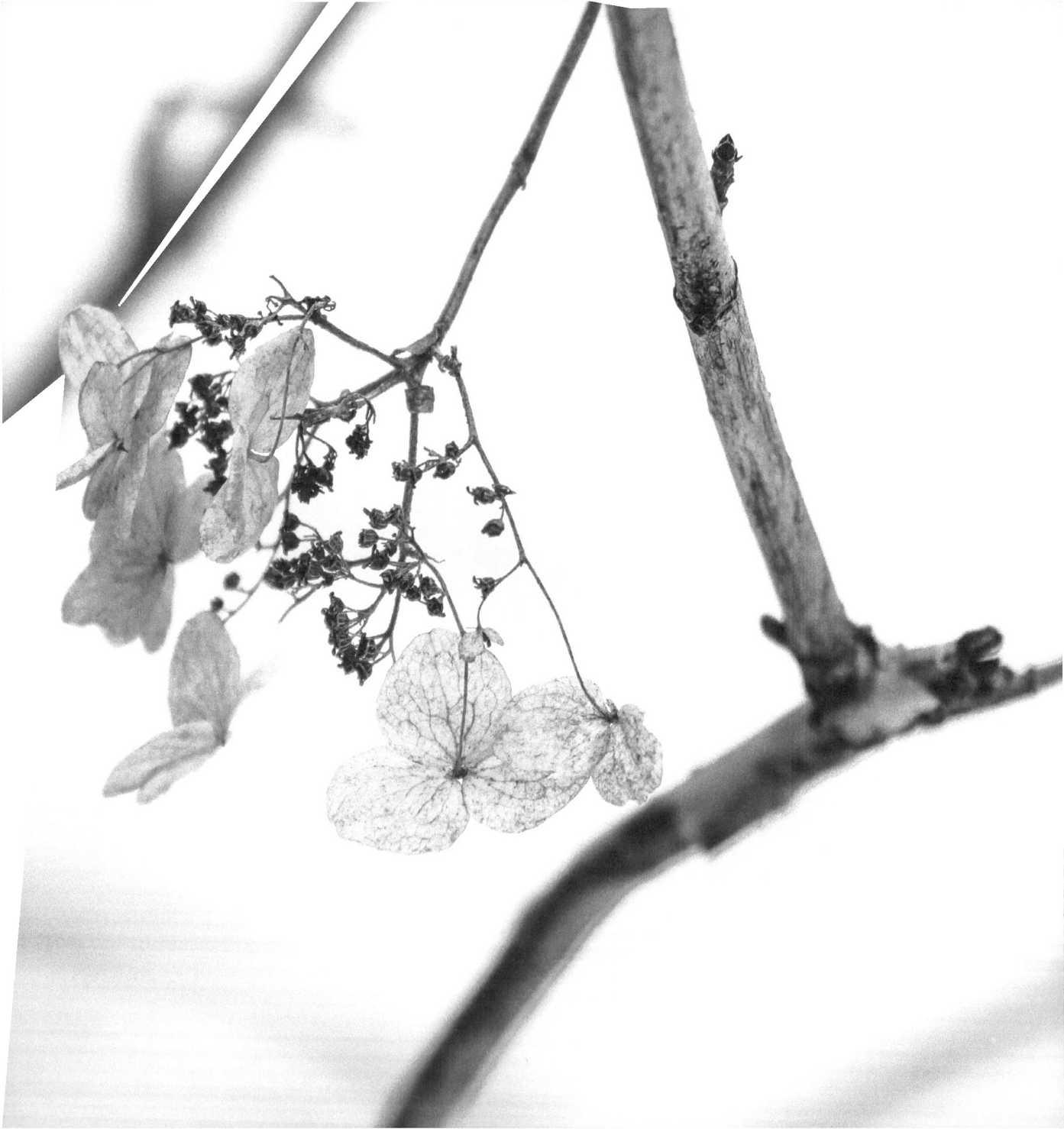

Widarto Adi

Widarto Adi (°1979, Jakarta, Indonesia) makes photos and drawings. Taking daily life as subject matter while commenting on the everyday aesthetic of middle class values, Adi wants to amplify the astonishment of the spectator by creating compositions or settings that generate tranquil poetic images that leave traces and balances on the edge of recognition and alienation.
His works are based on formal associations which open a unique poetic vein. By applying a poetic and often metaphorical language, he tries to develop forms that do not follow logical criteria, but are based only on subjective associations and formal parallels, which incite the viewer to make new personal associations. Widarto Adi currently lives and works in Albany, New York.

www.ingramcontent.com/pod-product-compliance
Lightning Source LLC
Chambersburg PA
CBHW050909180526
45159CB00007B/2852